# How To Do Something
# BESIDES
# WATCH TV

## A Survival Skills Book
## by Joy Berry

Managing Editor: Cathy Vertuca
Copy Editor: Annette Gooch
Contributing Editor: James Gough, M.D.
Writer's Assistant: Wendy Nicholson

Illustration Designer: Bartholomew
Inking Artist: Berenice Happé Iriks
Coloring Artist: Tom Rissacher

Art Direction: Communication Graphics
Design: Donna Fisher
Production: Canyon Fisher, Toni Douglass
Typesetting: Ananda

Published by Living Skills Press

When you are bored, you need to know about
- understanding boredom,
- taking care of responsibilities,
- finding out what you want to do,
- ideas for being physically active,
- ideas for being mentally active,
- ideas for being passive, and
- preventing boredom.

How do you feel when you are bored?

When you are bored, do you sometimes feel frustrated because you don't have anything to do?

When you need to find something to do, do you wonder. . .

This book can help you find positive things to do with your energy. It explains exactly what to do when you feel bored. It shows you how to come up with positive activities that are fun and interesting.

You might become **bored** when you can't think of anything interesting or exciting to do.

When you are bored, you might feel tired or restless.

When you are bored, you might feel as if you and your life are dreary and dull.

When you are bored, you might start feeling bad about yourself.

When you feel this way, you might want to do something destructive.

Doing something destructive is not a good way to handle boredom. It only causes you to get into trouble.

Therefore, it is not good to do anything that might hurt yourself or someone else.

It also is not good to do anything that might damage or destroy anyone's property.

You should not expect someone else to come up with something for you to do when you are bored.

It is up to you to make your life interesting and exciting. It is your responsibility to handle your boredom in a positive way.

You must decide what you are going to do when you feel bored.

It is important to choose something that will not get you into trouble.

When you are bored and need to think of something to do, begin by reviewing your responsibilities.

Decide whether you have any **chores** you need to do.

Decide whether you have any **promises** you need to fulfill.

Decide whether you have any **personal needs** you need to take care of.

Take care of any chores, promises, or personal needs **before** you do anything else!

### Avoid procrastinating!

Do not put off doing what needs to be done.

Handle your responsibilities first so that you can enjoy doing the other things you find to do.

Once you have fulfilled your responsibilities, you are ready to think about activities you might like to do.

Begin by deciding whether you want to be alone or with someone else.

Sometimes you might need or want to be alone.

Being alone can be relaxing. It can also be enjoyable.

Sometimes you might want to be with somebody else.

If you want to be with somebody else, do these things:

- ▪ Choose a person to be with.
- ▪ Ask permission from your parents to get together with the person.
- ▪ Talk with the person you want to be with. Ask if he or she can spend some time with you.

Once you know whether you are going to be alone or with somebody else, decide where you want to be.

Sometimes you might want to stay home.

If you are going to stay home, decide whether you want to be indoors or outdoors.

Sometimes you might not want to stay home.

If you want to go someplace away from home, do these things:

- Talk to your parents about places that are OK for you to walk or ride your bike to.
- Ask an adult to go with you if it is not OK for you to go someplace alone. Stay home if there is no adult who can go with you.

Once you have decided where you are going to be, decide what you want to do.

You might choose to do something that involves using your body or mind in an **active** way. This would include **physical activities** and **mental activities.**

Or, you might choose to do something **passive.**

Passive activities do not require you to use your body or your mind in an active way. They allow you to rest and relax.

Here are some ideas for being **physically active** when you are **outdoors:**

- Walk or jog.
- Practice or play a sport.
- Ride a bike or skateboard.
- Skate.
- Fly a kite.
- Throw a ball, Frisbee, or boomerang.
- Build something.
- Plant a garden.

Try to think of some more physically active things to do outdoors.

Make your own list.

Here are some ideas for being **physically active** when you
are **indoors:**

- Exercise.
- Practice tumbling.
- Dance.
- Pretend to be someone or something else and act it out with
  costumes and props.
- Play hopscotch using taped lines on the floor.
- Build a hideout or fort using things such as furniture, sheets, and boxes.
- Fly paper airplanes.
- Play games such as Twister, Simon Says, Follow the Leader, and Can
  You Do This?

Try to think of some more physically active things to do indoors.

Make your own list.

Here are ideas for being **mentally active** when you are **outdoors:**

- Work on an art project that might be too messy to do inside (sculpture, painting, papier-mâché).
- Observe something such as an insect or a plant. See what you can learn about it.
- Try to see things in your surroundings that you have never noticed before.
- See how many different sounds you can hear and identify in your environment.
- See how many different odors you can smell and identify.
- See how many different textures you can find and identify them.
- Organize a collection of things (such as rocks, leaves, or seeds).
- Conduct a scientific experiment that might be too messy to do inside.

Try to think of some more mentally active things to do outdoors.

Make your own list.

Here are some ideas for being **mentally active** when you are **indoors:**

- Read.
- Play a game such as solitaire or dominoes.
- Work on a puzzle, riddle, cipher, or code or make up your own.
- Create a work of art using crayons, colored chalk, colored pens, paints, or clay.
- Cook or bake something.
- Sew or mend something.
- Write something, such as a letter, poem, song, story, diary, or journal.
- Record yourself singing or speaking.
- Create something using materials you can find around the house such as straws, paper, paper clips, glue, fabric, or recycled containers and boxes.
- Play an instrument.
- Make a musical instrument and play it.

Try to think of some more mentally active things to do indoors.
Make your own list.

Here are some **passive** things you can do **outdoors:**

- Observe the clouds or other things in nature.
- Find a special place to be alone and sit quietly.
- Sit or lie down and let your thoughts wander.

Try to think of some more passive things to do outdoors. Make your own list.

Here are some **passive** things you can do **indoors:**

- Listen to music.
- Daydream.
- Take a catnap.
- Relax your mind and body.

Try to think of some more passive things to do indoors. Make your own list.

Having a plan can help prevent boredom.

Write down these questions.

- Whom do I want to be with?
- Where do I want to be?
- What do I want to do?

Answer the three questions when you are bored.

Make a list of things to do. The list should have three parts.

Part one of the list should include your **chores.**

Part two should include **places to go** (for times when you want to be away from home).

Part three of the list should include **things to do.**

Try to think of positive things to do.

Do not include any activities that might hurt other people or yourself.

Do not include any activities that might damage or destroy property.

Keep your lists of questions and activities in a handy spot.

Add to them as you discover new and exciting things to do.

Look over your lists when you need to find something to do.

With all the wonderful things you can do, you don't have to be bored if you don't want to be—it's completely up to you.